CADDO WAS ...

A SHORT HISTORY OF CADDO LAKE

by
Fred Dahmer

Library of Congress Catalog Card Number: 88-082564
ISBN: 0-944419-05-4

First Printing
October 1988
Collector's Edition

Cover Design: Rebecca Cason-Oates
Cover Water-coloring: Raleta Christian
Back Cover Photographs: by Loucille Dahmer

Caddo Was ...
By: Fred Dahmer

For information contact:

The Everett Companies
Publishing Division
P. O. Box 5376
Bossier City, LA 71171-5376

Phone: (318) 742-6240
LA (800) 826-6512   Outside LA (800) 423-7033

**Published in the United States of America
by: The Everett Companies
Publishing Division
813 Whittington Street
Bossier City, Louisiana 71112**

① 2 3 4 5

TABLE OF CONTENTS

CADDO WAS...

THE LIFE OF CADDO LAKE

Paragraph For A Friend

A good thing I have done in this life is make friends with Fred Dahmer. I know him as a person not given to grand claims about any subject, and especially not when the subject is himself. So I doubt he is going to say in this book how much he knows about Caddo Lake. My belief is that he knows more than anybody else alive about this mysterious, unique, and beautiful natural region. I could be wrong about that but I doubt it. Something I'm two-hundred per cent certain of is, nobody could love Caddo more than Dahmer does. He has lived a great part of his life on Caddo's shore. He has explored the lake's multitude of cypress channels, caught its fish, photographed its wildlife and its exquisite light and shadow. He has endured its floods, and its low-water times when his boat lay dry in its slip. He has also worried about the lake, and does still. Caddo's mysterious beauty has inspired a great lot of stories, some true and many nonsense. Fred Dahmer has a low tolerance for nonsense and I know one of the reasons for this book is, to present the facts about Caddo. Something to remember: When Dahmer says a thing about this lake, you can go and put it in the bank because it's true.

LEON HALE, August '88

(Leon Hale is a columnist for the Houston Chronicle and the author of six books.)

Author's Preface

"The history of Caddo Lake is colorful, complex and controversial." That's a quote from Chapter One of this little book of Caddo Lake history, and truer words were never written. Most of my knowledge of Caddo Lake legends and history were told to me by my great uncle, Jesse Ivir Carter, as I paddled the skiff while he cast enormous wooden plugs with an early "thumb brake" casting reel mounted on a stiff bamboo rod. Uncle Jesse was careful to tell me which of the stories he thought were true, and which were just fancy. He also taught me to respect the lake, the wildlife that depended on the lake, the game warden, and the laws he was there to enforce. My Aunt Frances, "Sis", brought her sketch pad and pencil along and opened my eyes to the beauty to be found in every nook and cranny of Caddo Lake. May they be granted the eternal joy of another Caddo Lake in the sky like the one we enjoyed when I was a very small boy.

The first *Caddo Was ...* was published in six installments, beginning with the June 1980 issue, Volume Two, of *The Greater Caddo Lake Association News*. By request, the six installments were repeated over the period of another year. Gerald Miller, editor of the paper, suggested that I should build on this "format" and make it into a small book. I told him that although I had planned revisions and new material, the typing would be too much for me, and I couldn't do it.

Several years later I was able to buy an "experienced" Commodore 64 and a word processing program, and the present edition is the result. Readers of the first editions will recognize this new and revised edition as a considerable improvement over the early ones which were written to meet publication deadlines.

Morley Hudson provided much help and advice during the time of rewriting, as well as proofreading and advice afterward. Wally Rausheck was invaluable as a reference source for names and incidents. Helene Smith and Ron Walker made many suggestions relative to publication format and marketing.

Leon Hale, Frank X. Tolbert, Randy Grothe, Karla Whitehead DeLuca, Bill Cockerill, Hermes and Mary Nye; have all contributed, perhaps unwittingly, to *Caddo Was* .... There are many others that I have not named because the list grows too long, but you know who you are. I thank each of you. I could not have finished without you.

Last but far from least I must acknowledge the unselfish support and loving encouragement of my family; my wife, Loucille, my four daughters, my sons-in-law, and my five grandchildren.

God Bless you all.

Fred Dahmer, 1986.

CADDO, the lake of mystery

CADDO WAS...

earth, and air, and water and from these there was Caddo Lake; with grace embellished; with all of life and beauty. The name of the first human to wander to Caddo's shore was probably never known to others. Perhaps it was before men had names; perhaps it was a woman drawn to a place of beauty. Named or not, that one is not forgotten. I think of him (or her) often... With envy...

Caddo Lake is the largest natural lake of fresh water within the state of Texas, but I must hasten to say that it is only about one half in Texas, and the remainder is in Louisiana. Located in the rolling hills and pine forests of northeast Texas, it is far removed from the dry and dusty plains often thought of as typical of Texas. As a matter of fact, the southwest corner of Arkansas is within twenty miles of Caddo. Almost all of the watershed supplying Caddo Lake is within Texas, the water draining through Little Cypress Bayou, Big Cypress Bayou, Black Cypress Bayou, and Jeems Bayou. Although the mouth of Jeems Bayou enters the lake just within Louisiana, the major part of its watershed is within Texas.

Now that I have pinned down the location of Caddo Lake for you, I must confess that from now on, it will be very difficult to make more than one unqualified statement on the subject of Caddo Lake, and I'll make it now: Caddo Lake is the most beautiful lake you will ever see.

I'm not alone in this assessment. First time visitors often literally gasp at that first view. Caddo is a lake of cypress trees, from the very young and small to the very old and large, and strangely, as you progress from Louisiana into Texas the older trees become more and more covered with hauntingly beautiful, gracefully draped, gently swaying Spanish moss. Although the moss is found at all parts of Caddo Lake, the truly luxuriant growth is mostly on

1

the Texas side of the lake centered around the Taylor Island, Mossy Brake, Carter and Clinton lake area.

The U.S. Army Corps of Engineers, in their 1973 report says that Caddo covers about 26,800 acres at 168.5ft. msl, however this varies considerably with the season and water level, since a large part of the lake is quite shallow, with gently sloping shores. Caddo is from 15 to 75 or more miles in length, depending on where you consider the head of the lake to be. I was once quoted as saying that Caddo was really three lakes, and started quite an argument thereby; but, in a sense it really is. The major tributary, Big Cypress, is navigable and was the route of the paddlewheel steamers all the way to Jefferson, Texas. Numerous small bayous and oxbows curve away from the channel on either side. Down river from Jefferson, the other two Cypress rivers, the Little and the Black have joined with the Big Cypress, and a few miles downstream, the river, or rivers form what must have been a river delta long ago. Today, it is a fantastic maze of interconnected waterways forming interlocked channels, lakes, ponds, bayous, oxbows, etc., separated by, and interspersed with, islands and brakes of Cypress trees. Continuing down stream a few miles, Caddo becomes a more conventional lake, more water than trees or brakes, somewhat deeper, and crossing into Louisiana. Near the lower end of Caddo Lake is Mooringsport, Louisiana. The Lake ends, today, three miles below Mooringsport at a low earthen dam. More about this later. I rest my case about the three lakes of Caddo: river, delta, open water.

The history of Caddo is colorful, complex, and controversial. The complete history of Caddo Lake has never been written. It exists in the minds, memories and "passed down" words of people. Many short writings have told and re-told these legends. It has often happened that the writers, with little or no experience of Caddo Lake, have not been able to discern the fine line between fact and fiction; while their sources have been overly concerned with contriving a fanciful tale. I have tried to make a mix of the very little source material available, the legends and oral history, filtered this with the physical evidence, and tempered all with my experiences of a life on Caddo Lake.

Nowadays, many people will say that Caddo Lake was formed in the earthquakes of 1811-12, the "New Madrid" quakes, which formed Reelfoot Lake at the same time. In my humble opinion this is about 80 to 90 percent WRONG. Here is the story I have put together, using my own method.

Long before the white man came, the area we now call Caddo Lake was a system of creeks, ponds, lakes and swamps interspersed with islands and hillocks of dry ground. In the rainy season there were good sized lakes, in the dry season it was a large swamp. Life of all kinds flourished. The indians which we now call Caddoes established semi-permanent villages on the low hillocks near the water. Each village, and there were many of them, consisted of a few houses made of saplings, skins, etc., with smooth hardpacked earthen floors. The indians hunted, fished, made weapons, pottery, burned the underbrush in the woods to keep it cleared for better hunting conditions, and generally led an idyllic peaceful life.

There are accounts from the 16th. and 17th. century by Spanish and French explorers of a "Laguna Madre" which some writers think may have been this place. Maybe so. We don't know because those explorers didn't say (or know) just where they were at the time. Whether it was, or was not, it could have been our Caddo Lake.

I have seen no accounts of any white people who may have been in this vicinity during the New Madrid quakes, but I consider it quite possible that the tremors were felt here. Trees may have been over-turned, and minor changes in the course of the Red River may have occurred. The Red River has changed course frequently without the help of an earthquake! We do know that in 1806 (BEFORE the New Madrid quake) the Freeman - Custis expedition, exploring the Red River for the U. S. Government, placed the Great Raft of the Red River above and below the present location of Shreveport. They reported that the raft completely obstructed the former channel of the Red, and was causing major flooding on all sides.

George W. Bonnell, in 1840, records in his journal having seen "Sodo Lake", a great body of water 20 miles long, and 8 miles wide. The name he gave it is from the indian name for it: "Tso'to". It is usually written "Soda Lake" to-day. Soda Lake was roughly between present day Mooringsport and Shreveport, about where Twelve Mile Bayou is now. This lake resulted from the overflowing of the Red River into what we now call Caddo Lake. It came through several channels in the general area around and between present day Oil City and Mooringsport. This was the "upper" end of the Soda Lakes and Cross Lake complex. This water returned to the nominal Red River channel at Shreveport. This same overflow of the Red River (around the upper Great Raft) caused the Big, Little, and Black Cypress rivers to "back up", and the lake thus formed was called "Fairy Lake" — our Caddo Lake. The name "Fairy" is often mis-spelled "Ferry", but U. S. Army Corps of Engineers reports used the name "Fairy Lake" during these early times.

Thus, Caddo Lake is both very ancient, and relatively modern. It was NOT formed overnight, nor was it anciently as large a lake as it presently is, except during periods of flood or high water. While the Red River rafts were in existence above Shreveport it had been possible, during most of the year, for river steamboats to reach Jefferson, Texas from ports on the Mississippi River, by way of Shreveport, Soda Lakes, Fairy Lake, and on up Big Cypress River. Landings were made on both North and South shores of Fairy Lake, in both Louisiana and Texas. It was during this period that the name Caddo Lake began to come into use to define the water complex of Fairy Lake.

When Shreveport business interests saw Jefferson prospering as the head of navigation, they lobbied successfully to get the raft above Shreveport removed, and this act "pulled the plug" on both Jefferson and Caddo Lake so far as the river steamboat traffic was concerned. Soda Lake was reduced to a drainage channel, and Caddo Lake became more or less a swamp area.

The indian legend, oft repeated, with variations, tells of the Great Chief who, in a vision, was told to move his tribe to high ground, from their village on low ground, to escape a deadly wall of water which would engulf the village overnight. The tribe fled to high ground in the vicinity of the present Texas Caddo State Park, and were saved from the water which covered their village overnight. When I was young, submerged indian house floors, and various Indian artifacts could be seen in the clear shallow water of Big Lake near Tar Island. This could have been the village of legend. The great artist and writer, Don Brown, recovered some of these artifacts from this underwater site. The site has since been lost under silt and aquatic vegetation.

Not too many years ago I helped Webster Hayner dig test holes along the South shore of Big Lake, and we found evidence of a similar indian village with house floors and artifacts. He was able to plot the house locations in the village, and carefully covered the test holes when finished. We also made diggings in Tow Head Island with inconclusive findings; possibly the location of a small hunting or fishing camp. The indian mound, for which Mound Pond is named, was widely known and dug into for many years. It has been levelled.

Drillers and geologists for the oil wells in Big Lake have reported that their core samples showed no evidence of any major earthquake in the area of the oil fields in and around Caddo Lake. I assume their tests would not disclose a minor subsidence of a few inches near the earth's surface.

When oil was discovered in the lake area just after the turn of the century, the oil companies found it very difficult to erect and operate their drilling rigs in what had been Caddo Lake, but which had returned to it's original swamp state with the removal of the Red River raft. They successfully lobbied to get a small dam built a short distance below Mooringsport, and thus restored enough depth of water in Caddo Lake to permit barge and work boat operation of their oil well activities, without permitting the return of navigation between Jefferson and Shreveport.

This dam site had been given a very low score in the U. S. Army Corps of Engineers report of 1874, due to unsuitable soil conditions. Business and politics prevailed over the engineering study, as often

The author on the way to Jefferson, Texas.   1928.

*The author with G. W. Witherspoon,
an old-timer on Caddo Lake.   1945.*

happens. Sure enough, eventually the dam developed major leaks as the unstable soil under it gave way. The dam has since been replaced, at about the same site, but with more modern technology. This dam forms the Caddo Lake of to-day.

The outstanding feature of Caddo Lake, it seems to me, is the number and size of the Bald Cypress trees. These trees are a marvelous clue to the natural history and development of Caddo Lake during the last few centuries. A count of the tree rings in a slab cut from the butt of a large cypress will prove its age. A cypress seed will take root only in damp ground. It will not naturally start rooting in dry ground, nor will it start growing in water more than an inch or two deep. The living Cypress trees which we observe IN the lake began life when they were NOT perennially covered with water, NOR were they on dry ground. The cypress brakes of to-day clearly define the former ponds, channels, creeks and swamp of the very old Caddo Lake.

When I bought my present place on Taylor Island there was a tiny cypress "sprout" about 18 inches high beside my boat slip. To-day, thirty years later, this tree is about 30 feet tall. The tree is not crowded by other trees, and I have pruned the lower branches a couple of times. I feel that this tree achieved about the maximum linear growth rate for the species, and that the RATE of growth in heighth will decline with each successive year as it approaches the maximum heighth for the species. The trunk is presently about 12 inches in diameter at the base. Perhaps, the trees that grow in dense cypress brakes cannot grow this quickly. In view of the slowing growth rate with age, I would estimate that a tree three or four feet in diameter at the base must be several centuries old. The seed from these huge old "Mother" trees fell to the water surface and were carried by wind, waves and currents to the shore line of the lake where they took root and grew into our present cypress trees.

Close examination of the popular large cypress wall clocks, which are sections of a cypress tree trunk, will show how close to-gether these rings are and how slowly the cypress grows in girth. The clock on your wall may be older than you realized!

All of these factors give us a clue to the size, appearance and development of Caddo Lake through the past several centuries to its present stage. Incidentally, just try to imagine Caddo without the cypress trees. What a dreary dismal scene it would be! With just water, it would be a lake; but, ONLY with cypress trees could it become our beloved CADDO LAKE!

Waterlilies and cypress, Caddo Lake.

Chapter 2

CADDO WAS...

BEYOND THE LAW !!

From the very first, western European civilization brought only strife, violence and turmoil to the Caddo Lake region which had been an idyllic home for the peace loving Caddo indians. To the early French and Spanish explorers this was a region where their rival claims overlapped, and they fought over this land; not for its own virtues, but for its strategic location.

The first Europeans to come to this area were the survivors of the French expedition led by La Salle in 1685. They reported a large tribe of friendly peaceable Indians living in a village near the bend of the Red River. The Indians said the name of their tribe was Kaddohadacho. The tribe was noted again in 1690 by the French explorer Tonti who was searching for the lost La Salle expedition. While the French were reaching this area from the East, The Spanish were arriving from the Southwest. Domingo de los Rios led a Spanish expedition to the vicinity of the Kaddohadachos in 1691. Later, in 1717, Spain made an unsuccessful attempt to establish a mission for the tribe. Both European nations soon began to establish missions and trading posts, as well as military bases to support their territorial claims, which overlapped here in the traditional home of the Kaddohadachos. The Indians were caught in the "no man's land" between the two rivals.

While the Christian nations fought each other for the homeland of the Caddoes, the heathen Indians tried to act as peacemakers between the two, whose explorers and missionaries they had welcomed and to whom they gave, freely, both food and friendship. It was the Caddo Indians who gave Texas its name. "Tejas" was their word for friend, and they used it so often the early explorers thought that it was the Indian name for this land.

CADDO WAS ...

The earlier Kaddohadachos tribe was a large "federation" of small "villages", covering many square miles. They were farmers, hunters, artisans and traders. An early traveler in this area reported that the Indian villages formed an almost continuous "avenue" from the bend of the Red River to Nacogdoches. They lived in peace with the other tribes and conducted a flourishing "business" with them, trading their handmade pottery, baskets,arrow heads, spear points, etc. for raw materials from distant lands. Other tribes had been able to trade with the Spaniards for horses, and the Caddoes soon acquired some of these. They were reported to be trading as far away as Illinois territory by the year 1715.

The good times were short-lived. The horses, guns, knives, fabrics, etc. brought by the Europeans were accompanied by whiskey, contagious diseases, duplicity and broken promises. The Caddoes declined rapidly in both power and population as both the Spanish and the French intruded more and more upon their home ground.

The Louisiana Territory was ceded by France to Spain, although many of the French people remained where they had settled. Then Louisiana was returned to France. Then the Louisiana Territory was purchased by the United States in 1803. During all of these years the boundary where it ran through the homeland of the Caddoes had been in dispute. No nation had been able to set up a system of civil law; not France, nor Spain, nor the United States, nor, the Caddo Indian Tribe.

When it became apparent to the wise old Caddo chiefs that the white man would continue to overrun their land, they agreed to a meeting with the United States agent to discuss a treaty for the sale of their land. Instrumental in arranging this meeting was Larkin Edwards who was a friend of the Indians and trusted by them. Although both parties to the treaty were willing for Edwards to act as translator and go-between, he knew that the Indians planned to give him some land, and therefore declined. His son was appointed, instead. Jehiel Brooks was agent for the United States. Tarshar was great Chief of the Caddoes, and with him was Under-chief Tsanninot and a council of twenty-three members. Colonel

Brooks was a master at high power salesmanship. He mentioned sums of money that sounded enormous to the poor Indians. Then he displayed wagons full of selected trade goods, that made the Indians' eyes shine. Then a detachment of the U.S. Infantry arrived and guards were placed around the Indians "to protect them" from the white men.

The treaty was signed on July 1, 1835. Tarshar, for the Caddo tribe, agreed to sell the United States all of their land for $80,000.00. Thirty thousand to be paid as soon as practicable in goods and horses, and $10,000.00 per annum for the next five years in money or goods at the Chief's option. The Chief agreed to remove all of the tribe from their former land at their own expense, within one year.

Included in the treaty was the reservation of one section of land, 640 acres, as a gift from the Caddo Indians to their friend, Larkin Edwards. The Caddoes also reserved four leagues of land located between the Red River and Bayou Pierre as a gift to the Grappe brothers, descendants of Touline, who had also been a friend and interpreter. Jehiel Brooks quickly bought this land from the Grappes. The treaty had been negotiated in a secrecy enforced by armed military guards, and the terms were kept secret until Brooks had completed his negotiations with the Grappes. Litigation resulting from the Brooks land claim involved the courts for many years. Larkin Edwards section is the site of Shreveport.

A few years ago, I returned from a day on the lake to find a woman photographer taking pictures of the lake from the lot next to mine, which was unoccupied at the time. She was of middle age, rather large, with long black hair, and wore a number of bracelets on her arms. Her camera was an expensive one, and her large camera bag, which lay open on the ground, contained an assortment of lenses. I decided she might be a Gypsy, and since I had taken many pictures from the same place, I complimented her choice of lens for the view. I remember her words: "I am a descendant of a princess of the Caddo tribes, and I am taking pictures of our ancestral homeland to show the children of our tribe".

Prior to the settlement of the boundary location, no government could claim and enforce jurisdiction over the area centering around Caddo Lake. People guilty of all sorts of crimes fled to the shores of the lake and the "neutral ground" to escape the law. Most were transient, but there were many who chose to settle here and start a new life. Others chose to continue their life of crime in this place where no law could reach them. Criminals ran rampant over the country-side, and law-abiding citizens lived in mortal terror. Old Monterey, on the shore of Monterey Lake, which is a part of Caddo Lake, became a center of criminal activity. It was noted for its race track, rooster fights, saloons and brothels; and boasted that it averaged at least one violent death per day. Travelers were ambushed, robbed and murdered. It is said that Jean Lafitte, the pirate, had close connections in Monterey, and may have visited there on several occasions.

Eventually, the law-abiding citizens could take no more. A vigilante group was organized. They called themselves "Regulators" to signify their intent to regulate the lawless. Predictably, the abuses of the Regulators became so bad that an opposing group, the "Moderators", was formed in order to moderate the Regulators. Woe betide the poor citizen caught in the middle who had chosen to join neither side. He was regulated when he encountered a Regulator, and perhaps in the same day, moderated when accosted by a Moderator. The trouble between the two groups eventually became a real war, with pitched battles, armed forts, and cannon. Few prominent men of the area escaped becoming involved.

Robert Potter, Secretary of the Navy of the Republic of Texas, who had settled with his wife, Harriet, on his land at Potter's Point was caught up in this feud and lost his life in a dramatic attempt to escape from "Old Rose" and his band of Regulators. They had surrounded the Potter home during the night, and one by one captured the household servants as they emerged in the early morning. When only Potter, Harriet and the small children were left inside they realized what was happening. Although Harriet pleaded with him to stay and fight it out with Old Rose, Potter decided to make a run for the lake which was not far down the bluff from the house and swim to one of the islands in the lake. Carrying his rifle, he dashed from the house to the water's edge, placed his rifle against a tree and dove into the lake. Rose and his men followed and when Rose saw Potter's rifle so handy, he raised it and fired the one shot at the now distant Potter.

Rose and his men then left without harming Harriet or the children. Although Harriet took the boat and searched the islands and cypress brakes, she could not locate Potter. His body floated to the surface of the lake a day or two later. There was one rifle hole in the back of his head. Harriet buried Potter on the bluff near the house overlooking the lake he loved so dearly.

When I last visited the site of Potter's grave, the little cemetary and some flowers not native to this area were all that showed any sign that men had once trampled this earth. This visit was made shortly after I returned home from service in WW2, about 1946. The graves of the Potter daughter, and a Potter servant were still visible. The remains of Potter himself were removed in 1936 by the state of Texas as part of the Texas Centennial and re-interred in the state cemetary at Austin. The area has now been divided into house lots with streets, power lines, etc., and I have not been back to see if the little cemetary is still there.

The lawlessness of the neutral Ground was clearly out of control. An expedition of 500 militiamen under Gen. James Smith, plus an impassioned plea by Sam Houston resulted in a lessening of the armed conflicts about 1844, although personal animosities remained for many years.

The border dispute was settled in 1849 and a survey line run through Caddo Lake. The Republic of Texas, through treaty, had become one of the United States. Law was established, and order gradually restored. However, the heritage of lawlessness left its stain on Caddo Lake. Even unto recent times the lake has been exploited by bootleggers, illegal fish and game poachers, timber thieves, land thieves, gamblers and others who make use of the devious channels and remote hideaways to carry on activities beyond the law.

The law officials and game wardens on Caddo Lake have been men of wit and courage, and their lives were every bit as colorful and as full of danger as that of any western marshal. Among the noted game wardens that I recall were Bun Roe, Walter Leak Akin, F. O. Spearman, Albert Hall, Roscoe Rausheck, and Allen Ellis, and of course there were many others. All were expert marksmen and fearless in the performance of their duty; but, they were always greatly outnumbered. The nature of Caddo Lake favored the violators. I knew an outlaw commercial fisherman who said he would never kill a waterbird for bait because they would always squawk and fly away when the game warden tried to catch him running the traps at night; an aquatic watchdog worth preserving. It was Allen Ellis who once showed me just what could be done with a short two-inch barrelled Smith & Wesson .38 Special on a tin can which he had me throw into the air. Firing from the hip, he hit the can twice in the air, and then pushed it along the ground with each shot until the cylinder was empty. It was just a small evaporated milk can, too. The remains weren't worth saving. I was impressed. I remember that he had used a grinder or file to remove the front of the trigger guard so it wouldn't get in the way of his trigger finger.

When you go to the movies, if you stay long enough the program comes around to "where you came in". Maybe it's the same in the history of Caddo Lake. Recently I became involved in a new boundary line dispute in Caddo Lake. It seems that while we weren't looking, the whimsical cartographers of the Federal government had moved the Harrison-Marion County line on the official U.S. maps, where it runs through Caddo Lake. This boundary line had been established by an act of the Texas Legislature, which plainly stated that the line was the center of the channel of Big Cypress where it runs through Caddo Lake to the Texas-Louisiana State line. The map-makers had snatched the line and hidden it away in Alligator Bayou. This seems unimportant, at first glance, but it brought on a case before judge and jury at which I was called to testify as an expert witness. Taxable land had been changed from Marion County to Harrison County. Game laws in the two counties differ. Jurisdiction of the Marion County court is diminished while that of Harrison County is enhanced. I enlisted the aid of a news reporter and the latest maps I have seen have moved the line back, closer to where it belongs. They've got it in Jackson's Arm now! I wish they would let me show them where it should be. The bed I sleep in has been within a hundred or so yards of it for over forty years.

Entrance to a hidden pond in Caddo.

CADDO WAS ...

Lover's Lane in Mossy Brake, Caddo Lake.

Chapter 3

CADDO WAS...

STEAMBOATS !!

The coming of the steamboats to Caddo Lake seems to me to have been the crowning achievement of an era of mechanical invention and human daring fully the equal, for its time, of our modern manned space ventures. The navigation of our western rivers was made practicable by Henry Miller Shreve, and to understand the presence of steamboats on Caddo it is necessary to understand a little of his life and activities. Although his work greatly affected Caddo Lake and all of this region, it is doubtful that he ever saw the lake.

Henry was next to the youngest of the six children of Colonel Israel Shreve, a veteran of the American Revolution. He had a child's fascination for the boatyards and the riverboatmen's tales of adventure on the Mississippi. He was still in his teens when he joined the crew of a keelboat headed for New Orleans. Shreve was a fast learner and a hardworker. By the time he was 21 he had built his own flatboat. At 23 he made $11,000.00 on one trip by using his boat to haul lead ore from the mine at Galena, Illinois to New Orleans, where he transshipped the cargo by boat to Philadelphia. A year later Shreve took the opportunity to examine the Fulton steamboat NEW ORLEANS, which had been brought down the river by Nicolas Roosevelt.

(This was the first steamboat ever on the Mississippi, and by this demonstration the Fulton-Livingston interests hoped to obtain an exclusive charter for the use of steamboats on the Mississippi, as they had done on the Eastern rivers. It was during this trip, in the Winter of 1811-1812, just as the steamer neared New Madrid, that the great New Madrid earthquake occurred. This was a horrendous earthquake; the worst in the recorded history of the Eastern United States, and the steamer with its crew and passengers was very, very lucky to survive. Could this quake possibly have created Caddo Lake at this time? Although it is known to have created Reelfoot Lake, which is said to have some similarities to Caddo Lake, and although many people believe that Caddo Lake was created by this event, it is my personal conviction that Caddo Lake was gradually forming for hundreds of years before 1812.

Henry Shreve examined this first steamer on the Mississippi very carefully. He determined that the Watts low pressure steam engine was too weak and too heavy for satisfactory use in the swift currents and shallow waters of the Western Rivers, the round-bottomed hull sat too deeply in the water. Shreve felt he could design a much more suitable boat. After six years of running his own flatboats and keelboats, Shreve had put away some money, and he associated himself with Daniel French, inventor of a high pressure steamboat engine. Eventually, French built a steamer, the ENTERPRISE, incorporating his high pressure engine, and, with Shreve as Captain, loaded it with ordnance stores for New Orleans. The ENTERPRISE arrived at New Orleans two weeks after leaving Pittsburg. She was immediately attached by the Fulton Group, but Shreve was able to post bail. The siege of New Orleans was underway. General Jackson commandeered both the ENTERPRISE and Shreve for military service, which included a trip up the Mississippi to tow down river some flatboats loaded with military stores, and two trips up the Red River, carrying women and children to safety, away from the battle. Shreve brought the ENTERPRISE back to Louisville by the end of May. The boat had performed flawlessly, and Shreve was a military hero. Several firsts were accomplished: the first barge tow by steamboat on the Mississippi, the first steamboat to navigate the Red River, the first steamboat evacuation of a city under military siege, and the first steamboat to make a return voyage up the Mississippi under its own steam power. All the way back Shreve dreamed of the improvements he would design into his own boat.

First, he would name the boat after his father's commander in the Revolution: The WASHINGTON. Next, the hull would be patterned after the proven design of a Mississippi River keelboat, flat and wide, curving bluntly to a point in front. It would have no cargo hold, but would be decked over, and the cargo would be carried on the deck. The engines would be on top of the deck also, one engine for each paddlewheel, so the wheels could be operated independently. The high pressure engines would use fixed horizontal cylinders with cutoff valves, and with connecting rods on each piston to drive the paddle wheels. The four high pressure boilers, built with tube flues, would be mounted on the guards, two on each side. The paddlewheels would be set well aft on each side for more efficient operation when under way. The cabin would be almost the full length of the hull, and would be two decks high, with the wheelhouse on top. Because of the shallow hull design, he would build a heavy timber "truss" rising fore and aft about ten feet above the deck, on the centerline above the keel, to strengthen the hull and control the "limberness".

Shreve hired George White of Wheeling, West Virginia to build the boat, and supervised every detail of the construction. He had his friend, Daniel French build the engines just as he had planned them. French tried to get Shreve to change his overall design, but Shreve refused to take any advice. The local experts predicted everything from total failure to complete disaster. The work was finished in a remarkably short time, and the moment of truth arrived. In two trial runs Shreve put the boat through its paces. It was a howling success! Shreve quickly put the boat into commercial service — and one of the high pressure boilers blew up, killing a number of the crew. Shreve himself was in the pilot house and was blown over board, but escaped serious injury. The damage was soon repaired and the WASHINGTON put back in service. Henry Shreve's first western river steamboat was a remarkable success. It led the way for thousands of copies, and literally changed the history of our country — and of Caddo Lake.

The Fulton-Livingston interests and their obsolete steam boats were no longer able to compete for an exclusive franchise on the Mississippi, or its tributaries, and withdrew their suit against Daniel French and Henry Shreve. There remained only one real obstacle to free use of the river by western type steamboats, and that was a natural one. Over the centuries, thousands of trees had fallen from eroding banks and been carried by the water currents to varying distances downstream, until one end snagged on the bottom of the river. The riverboatmen classified these fallen giants into "planters" and "sawyers", depending upon whether the free end of the trunk "sawed" to and fro in the water currents. Partially submerged, the snags were difficult to avoid. They could, and often did, rip out the bottom of the steamer, causing great loss of life and property. The Corps of Engineers estimated it would take many millions to remove these snags, but eventually gave up when no one would take the contract. Henry Shreve put his mind to this problem. He designed a snagboat especially for this purpose, got the government to build it for him, named it the HELIOPOLIS, steamed to Plum Point, the most dangerous concentration of snags on the river, and in eleven hours had cleared the river channel. In less than two years Shreve removed all of the old snags from the entire length of the Mississippi, and the snagboat easily removed the fresh ones as they formed.

Shreve wasn't long out of a job. For as far back as the first recorded exploration, the channel of the Red River had been totally blocked for a distance of one hundred and fifty miles by a great raft of fallen trees. The river had been forced out of its normal channel and was flooding on both sides of the channel. Congress appropriated $28,000.00 to improve the river, and a party of engineers started out. They soon decided that if it was even possible to remove the raft it would take two or three million dollars. The call went out for Henry Shreve, and he started with what was left of the twenty-eight thousand dollars. In two and a half months he cleared seventy miles of the Great Raft. He stopped when the money ran out. When Congress would give him a little more money, he would work some more. Each time he ran out of money and stopped, the raft would begin to form again, but eventually he finished the contract in 1838 at a total cost to the government of $300,000.00. He had arrived at what would soon be known as Shreve Town, — and a little later, as Shreveport.

While the western river steamboat designed by Shreve was a fast and cheap form of transportation compared to the wagon or cart, it was not an unmixed blessing. It ushered in an era of terrible disasters, such as had never been known before. The boilers on the main deck were among, and close to, their own fuel, the ship's cargo, which often consisted of highly inflammable cotton, tallow, hay, etc., —and the passengers. The boilers operated at higher pressures than was safe for the technology and engineering of the time. Also, the wide flat-bottomed, low-sided hull, built entirely of wood, was inherently quite weak (compared to a regular ship's hull) and required the rope and cable trussing to stiffen it. To put it bluntly: if the boat didn't catch afire, and the boiler didn't blow up, it likely sank when it hit a snag!

When everything went well, however, it was an elegant and swift way to travel; far more comfortable than slow and bumpy wagons, or even stagecoaches. Safe from attack by marauding indians, the steamers even carried their own full time dining room, ball room and bar, with a soft bed to rest in at night. With experienced pilots aboard, and weather permitting, many steamers continued to operate at night. So, although Shreve's "invention" became the most dangerous means of transportation that has been known to man, it was very popular, and thousands of the type were built ranging from small and crude ones to the legendary large and elegant "floating palaces".

Everywhere, brave steamboat captains (you had to be brave to even get near a steamboat!) were pushing their steamers further and further into unknown waters, and soon Captain John Rives brought his steamer into Caddo Lake. This was about 1845. (I cannot confirm this date and it may have been earlier). Others soon followed, and eventually reached the little settlement of Jefferson on Big Cypress Bayou. They had opened up a lush new country of great plantations, cattle, and natural resources beyond measure.

Little did they realize that their steamers were passing right over the greatest resource of all — underground pools of oil and gas; literally, under their very paddlewheels. There were, also, great forests of virgin pine, tall and straight, oak, hickory and walnut trees, plentiful fish, flocks of ducks and geese sufficient to darken the sky as they passed overhead, black bear, deer, squirrels, rabbits, giant mussels bearing freshwater pearls; Caddo Lake must have seemed to these men like paradise unfolding before the prow of their boats.

But remember, the discovery of Caddo Lake by steam came about because Henry Miller Shreve used up his allocation of government money at Canes's Bluff and decided to quit and found a town, which would become the head of navigation on the Red River, thus creating a nice investment possibility for himself and others. He bought a section of land here.

Shreve went back down the river looking for more government work, believing that the great raft above Shreveport would stop all further navigation, and not realizing that the raft he left would, of itself, open a channel for steamers to enter Caddo Lake, and even by-pass the raft to go further upstream on the Red River, even to enter Texas through Big Cypress River.

Although the Caddo Lake route was somewhat seasonal, depending on the water levels in the Cypress River and the Red River, there was often more water than less at the level required for operation by rather large steamboats. In addition to the water dammed by the log raft itself, we must remember that in those early days our forests had not been clear cut, and the area of cultivated land was comparatively small. As a result, the rainfall run-off was much slower than at present, and this maintained a higher level of water for a longer time than we would expect from the same amount of rain to-day.

Much has been written about the days of steamers on Caddo Lake. These were glorious times when the frontiers of our nation were being won. Many brave men and women were making a new life in Texas. Fortunes were being made in cotton, timber, cattle, iron and real estate. Jefferson became the second largest port in the state of Texas, exceeded only by Galveston. Each year brought thousands of travellers and millions of dollars of freight through Jefferson.

Although Shreveport prospered and grew vigorously, it was not the head of navigation and did not get the booming prosperity enjoyed by Jefferson.

Jackson's Arm, Caddo Lake.

*These cypress trees saw the steamboats
come and go through Caddo Lake.*

Chapter 4

CADDO WAS...

PATHWAY OF THE PADDLEWHEELS!!

Through the initiative of Henry Shreve the ponderous Fulton steamboat had metamorphosed into the powerful western river steamer, eminently suitable for use on the Mississippi River and its tributaries. Basically, the boat was simple enough to be built in small boatyards without elaborate facilities or overly skilled workmen. However, the larger boatyards specialized in speedy passenger and mail steamers which quickly led to the development of the elegant, overly ornate "floating palaces", with comfortable staterooms, sumptious main cabin and gourmet cuisine.

Many of these steamers were owned by their captains, who took great pride in them; and, as more and more boats were placed in service, the captain-owners raced each other for fame as well as business. Certain steamer captains were soon well known for their skill and daring, idolized by young and old alike.

As these famous men and their elegant boats took over the Mississippi River trade, the smaller steamers began to look elsewhere for business, in the tributaries and bayous of the great river. When Shreve removed the Great Raft of the Red River, they soon found their way into our Caddo Lake, named "Fairy Lake" on some maps of that time. There is some evidence to indicate that steamers may have entered Caddo even before removal of the raft was completed to Shreveport, since they might have gone around the raft when the river was up.

Because almost all of the Western steamers burned wood for fuel, they were able to explore Southern rivers without fuel restriction. This made it possible for them to operate freely in our Caddo Lake area, getting fuel whenever they needed it from woodyards along the shore. They preferred good dry hardwood when they could get it, but nearly anything flammable would do in a pinch.

The resinous heartwood found in pine trees, especially in the stumps and roots of a cutover pine forest was called "fat wood" and was used whenever instant heat or a "bright" fire was required. It made a quick and hot fire, and was often used as a "fire starter".

In the very early days it was burned in a cast iron basket with a reflector behind, atop the wheelhouse, as a search light when needed for night travel. Although the steamers often traveled at night in familiar waters, the lights were seldom used or required while under way. They were helpful, however, when night landings and loading operations were being made.

Can you imagine a dark and windy night in February with a paddle wheel steamer, boiler fireboxes flaring open on the main deck, "searchlight" streaming flames and embers above the wheelhouse; all amidst a cargo of hay, cotton, gunpowder, etc. on the same main deck with the fuel and "fat wood", slowly picking its way through Broad Lake, heading for Swanson's Landing?

Just such a situation confronted the "Mittie Stephens" on the night of February 11, 1869, with one hundred souls aboard. Just before midnight, in the vicinity of Swanson's Landing, Time ran out for the "Mittie" as the deck cargo began to smoke and flames suddenly engulfed the entire deck. Amidst screams and cries of passengers and crew, the captain guided his flaming vessel toward shallow water and the shore, but many terrified souls jumped overboard prematurely and were drawn into the churning paddlewheels. At least sixty lives were lost. When I was a boy there were several abandoned or wrecked steamboat hulks visible in and around the Lake. There are said to be some still, under the surface. I never saw any wreckage of the "Mittie Stephens", however. I assume that everything of any value or use had been removed.

Actually, before the end of the 1840's we find steamer traffic in Caddo Lake to be heavy, and Port Caddo fairly well established as a freight and mail terminal, and customhouse. Harrison County had voted funds for a road (the "Old Port Caddo Road", sometimes called "The Old Stagecoach Road") to Marshall. The collection of Custom duties seems to have been more theoretical than actual, however, as the Port Caddoans disposed of the collectors as fast as they were sent, and the County Sheriff said he was unable to protect them.

One of the larger steamers calling at Port Caddo was "The Caddo", advertised as an elegant vessel with a capacity of 1,550 bales of cotton, 150 feet long, 31 feet in beam, and 6 1/2 feet depth of hold, with two engines to drive the sternwheel. The cylinders of the engines were advertised as having a bore of 17 1/2 inches, with a 7 foot stroke! Other steamers calling at Port Caddo were the "Indian" and the "Nicholas Biddle". These were reported to have been at Port Caddo in 1836, which was two years before Henry Shreve finished clearing the Great Raft to Shreveport.

After leaving Shreveport, the steamers used several alternate routes to enter Caddo Lake, depending on the water level and vagaries of the channels caused by log jams, uprooted trees, etc., and the landings to be made. One route was through Cross Bayou and Cross Lake before entering The Sodo Lake chain of lakes. Another route was through Twelve Mile Bayou and the Sodo Lakes. Before entering Caddo Lake proper, they had to traverse a treacherous bit of water , shallow and with shifting channels, known as "Albany Flats". This area was created by the accumulation of sediment from the Red River which found a natural settling basin here. In places the sediment was sufficiently deep to have covered mature trees so that only their tops were visible.

Navigation was possible , generally, for eight or nine months in an average year. The dry months were not wasted as the low water permitted improvements at the landing places, construction of wharves and piers, as well as replenishment of the woodyards. This was a time to clear the smaller favorite channels of fallen trees, logs and stumps.

Almost all of the steamers were "locals", and would stop for any plantation where they had business. The arrival of a steamboat at a plantation landing was a joyful occasion for the Caddoans, as they brought letters, news, gifts and special purchases from the outside world. Some of the better known landings in Caddo Lake were: Bonham's Landing, Monterey Landing, Swanson's Landing, Benton's

Landing, Willowson Woodyard, Port Caddo and Jefferson, which, in the 1850's came into its own as the head of navigation on Cypress River for entry into the State of Texas.

So many steamboats were entering and traversing Caddo Lake that in 1852 a group of men obtained a charter for a railroad to run from Swanson's Landing to Marshall. This was the second railroad in Texas, and was chartered with the grand name of TEXAS WESTERN. Construction was begun as quickly as possible with the laying of track to Waskom and westward to Marshall. The fledgling railroad suffered through all of the difficulties that could be expected of the times and place, but ended up with the track just a mile short of Marshall. The charter had set a deadline for operation of the first train, and the steam locomotive had not arrived in time. (It never did arrive.) The story is often related that a Mr. Charley Hynson hitched a team of oxen to a train of three flatcars and started for Marshall. The team of oxen pulled the string of flat cars up the hills and on the level, and then rode the flat cars down the hills. The charter was saved. Through a series of charter acquisitions and sales it can, and has, been shown that this little railroad, which started life at Swanson's Landing on Caddo Lake was the beginning of the TEXAS AND PACIFIC railroad, years later purchased by MISSOURI PACIFIC, and only recently by UNION PACIFIC, which still runs to Marshall. —-But not to Swanson's Landing!!!

Steamers arriving at Jefferson numbered into the hundreds. They came in all sizes and types: from small to large, from dirty to elegant, from cargo to passenger and mail packet. Their names were typical of river boats everywhere: "Edinburgh", "C. H. Durfee", "John G. Sentell", "John T. Moore", "Fleeta", "R. T. Briarly", "Mittie Stephens", "Jessie K. Bell", "Lotus No.3", "Thirteenth Era", "Era No.9", "Era No.10", "New Era", "Col. A. P. Kouns", "Katie P. Kouns", and on and on. I can envy the passengers on one of the finer steamers as they chugged smoothly over the water on a summer evening watching the sun setting across Broad Lake and then the moon rising over Big Green Brake, on their way to a new life in Texas.

The history of Jefferson is very properly a part of Caddo Lake history. They are inseparable, but that part of the story has been better told by more able writers.

View of the commercial waterfront of Jefferson, Texas in June 1928.

The quiet water of Caddo Lake was literally being churned to a frenzied froth by the paddlewheels of more and more steamboat traffic. The boats were becoming larger and faster as competition increased, especially for the cotton business. As the boats increased in size the cargos became larger and larger, and the shipping charges became smaller and smaller. This encouraged the plantation owners to produce more and more cotton. The size of the cotton carriers was expressed in the number of bales of cotton they could carry. Some of the larger boats to ply between Jefferson and New Orleans could carry from one to two thousand bales. Smaller boats would so exceed their capacity that some overturned and sank. The passenger steamers were busy, too, as thousands of immigrants chose to seek a new life in Texas. Many of the steamers were especially built and equipped to haul the longhorn cattle which were beginning

*Scene at Dallas Caddo Club, Uncertain, Texas. June 30, 1930.
Left, the "Waltonian"; center, the "Hello World" (owned by W. K. Henderson of KWKH radio).
The smaller inboard boat in the right foreground is the "Sunshine",
later owned by the author and his wife.*

to arrive from the West. These were the days to remember for the Caddoans. Business of all kinds was booming, and as goods of all kinds became plentiful, so did the money to buy them become plentiful. These good days lasted until the Civil War, when the North blockaded Southern trade efforts to get their cotton to the textile mills.

The steamer traffic through Caddo Lake, although much reduced in volume, continued through the war. It was considered vital for the movement of both military and civilian supplies to the rest of the Confederacy. The iron ore of East Texas was being smelted and the iron fabricated at an iron works in Jefferson. Ammunition was being manufactured in Marshall and at other nearby ordnance plants. Cattle hides were made into leather, and then converted into harness and saddles throughout the area. However, the cotton producers were prudently hiding their bales of cotton, since they could not get them to the textile mills. As Northern forces gradually took over the Mississippi River many steamboats fled up the Red River to escape capture and they were hidden in smaller bayous and lakes, including Caddo. Two steamboats were converted to gunboats at Shreveport, and one made a daring escape after the capture of New Orleans. It was finally run aground after it had passed New Orleans and was almost into the Gulf of Mexico.

After the war, steamboat traffic in Caddo Lake continued to increase until 1873, when the remaining portion of the Great Red River Raft, the part above Shreveport, was removed. The water level in Caddo Lake and the Soda Lakes gradually became lower and lower. This was a slow process, first evidenced by a reduction in the length of time each year during which navigation was possible. However, the far-reaching effect of the raft removal had apparently been foreseen by the U. S. Corps of Engineers. Their report of 1874 on Caddo Lake shows that the damage to navigation on Caddo Lake was irreparable. Several studies by different engineers were made, involving dams, gates and canals at various locations, but all reached the same conclusion: there simply was no reasonable way to restore even a semblance of navigation on Caddo Lake as it had been. As the duration of the high water season dwindled to only a month or two each year, steamboat operation was no longer profitable, and by the end of the century, the resonant charm of steamboat whistles as they rounded Devil's Elbow echoed no more across the water of Caddo Lake.

An unexpected result of removing the raft was that the Red River at Shreveport also became too shallow to support navigation as it once had been. Caddo Lake and Soda Lake had acted as an enormous self regulated reservoir which had drained slowly enough back into the Red River, just above Shreveport, to help maintain the water level in the Red River at Shreveport, as well as in the Cypress River. The removal of the Great Raft was a tragedy, from which Jefferson and all of our area has never recovered. The cost of this error by the Federal Government must be counted as more than the billions of dollars in lost revenues. Now the government is spending more billions in tax money in an effort to restore the navigation which was once ours without cost.

Meanwhile, Shreveport has constructed a low dam on Twelve Mile Bayou to replace in a small way the great chain of lakes which was called "Sodo Lake". Sodo is the anglicized version of the Caddo Indian name which sounds like "Tso'to" and which translates to "Water thrown up into the drift along the shore by the wind"... Alas, the drift, and the windswept sparkling water is now only a memory. Pass it on!

Chapter 5

CADDO WAS...

ROBERT AND HARRIET'S!

No story of Caddo Lake would be complete without mention of Robert Potter and his contemporaries. The story of his life rivals the wildest tales of fiction. Looking back on those events of a century and a half ago, it seems inevitable that Robert Potter should be drawn to Caddo Lake, and that his life should end in the amber water of Caddo Lake, as violently as he had lived it.

Potter was born in 1799 in Williamsburg, North Carolina. When he was 15 he decided that he would serve his country, and applied for a midshipman's berth in the U. S. Navy. He was accepted, and served six years, with the exception of a one year leave to assist his parents. He resigned from the Naval service in March 1821, and returned to Halifax, N.C., where he read law in the office of Thomas Burges. He ran for the House of Commons in 1824, and again in 1825, and was elected in 1826, in a very light vote.

Potter was a gifted orator and a shrewd politician. He would speak on any occasion, and usually gained the support of his listeners, although his sharp tongue usually infuriated the opposition. He was a populist and introduced a number of measures to further the educational system of his state, and to help the common man. Potter married a Miss Pelham in 1828, and was elected to the United States House of Representatives in November 1828.

In Washington, Potter's character developed the dichotomy that would rule the rest of his life. In his public life he became a leader, a defender of the people, an astute statesman. His private life was an ethical and moral mess! He was a handsome, charming "lady-killer", without conscience or moral restraint, a gambler to excess, given to violence, and a cunning schemer. Although he had a wife in North Carolina, he became "engaged" to a Washington girl. Realizing the awkwardness of his situation, when he returned home he accused his wife, apparently falsely, of adultery with her minister and also her cousin. When this accusation was greeted with some skepticism, he assaulted the two men, separately, and maimed them in a manner he deemed appropriate to the alleged offense.

Potter was arrested, tried and sentenced to two years in jail. His crime received wide publicity, and for many years this type of maiming was called "Potterizing". Potter served his sentence, reading and writing poetry while in jail, and upon release made the long journey to Texas to get away from those who knew him too well.

Naturally he headed for the "Neutral Ground", where no man was questioned about his past. Texians were just beginning to declare their independence of Mexico. Potter, in Nacogdoches, decided to run as a delegate to the Constitutional Convention. A group of volunteer soldiers had just arrived and declared their right to vote in the election. Local citizens were resisting, claiming the soldiers had not met the residency requirements. Potter saw his chance and made a fiery speech in favor of the soldier's right to vote. His brilliant oratory prevailed, and of course the grateful soldiers voted for him. I told you he was a shrewd politician!

Because of his previous naval experience, Potter was appointed Secretary of the Navy of the Republic of Texas, and he directed the Texas Navy's operations during the war of independence. Several ships were available to the Navy, and it was generally agreed that he did well with the forces at his disposal.

It was at this time that he met Harriet Moore Page, who, with her infant children, was fleeing before the advancing Mexican Army. Potter assisted her, personally, placing her aboard his flagship at Galveston, and promising to see that she was returned to her grandparents home in Kentucky as soon as his duties permitted.

There must be times when Fate leaves nothing to chance! Bringing these two people together was roughly the same as dropping a lighted match in an open keg of gunpowder. Their life together is beautifully told in Harriet's own words in her autobiography, "THE HISTORY OF HARRIET AMES". It is the basis of the novel, LOVE IS A WILD ASSAULT, by Elithe Hamilton Kirkland.

View from the high bluff on Potter's Point looking across Caddo Lake in the direction of Swanson's Landing, the scene that Harriet Potter describes in her autobiography. The Potter cemetery is nearby. Photo by the author, 1948.

If Harriet's autobiography is authentic, and it certainly seems so, she must have been quite a gal; good looking, smart, literate, level headed, fastidious in dress, yet skilled in dressmaking, a loving and capable wife and mother. According to Harriet, her husband, Solomon Page, had abandoned her and their two children on the Texas prairie with no food, and far from help.

Potter had offered her his protection and return to her family; however, when he secured passage from New Orleans, it was aboard a river steamboat bound for the Red River, and Caddo Lake. Harriet soon realized this wasn't the usual way to get to Kentucky, and so they got off at Alexandria to go overland. Undiscouraged, Potter led the way through the countryside, and they ended up on the Sabine River! Here they were united in a "bond marriage". Potter had convinced her that since she and Solomon Page had not been married by a priest her marriage was not legal in Texas; but, the "bond marriage" was, or would be, as soon as the legislature of the new republic could convene. He also told her that he had secured several thousand acres of land on Caddo Lake, reputedly the most beautiful place in Texas, and was building a home for them there.

Harriet's first sight of their new home on Potter's Point, Caddo Lake, is eloquently told in her own words:

"A place more beautiful than Potter's Point it would be impossible to imagine. I never tired of admiring the scenery that lay about my new home. Our home stood upon a jutting promontory that rose into a hill set in the midst of one of the grandest timber belts in Texas. The level timber lands circled about us, while, for more than two hundred feet, a steep bank overlooked the most romantically beautiful lake that I've ever beheld. For eight miles one could look across to the opposite shore over a great sheet of sparkling water that washed up into the white beaches below the cliff and sang a soft song that the spirits of the forests caught up and carried on unseen wings into the forest's depths and tangled music in the meshes of the lofty tree tops."

Texas had won her fight for independence and Potter was one of the heroes, an elected representative of his district, and prominent in the organization of the government. He introduced a bill giving four acres of Texas land for the establishment of Marshall University. He also introduced land reform bills to save the young nation's land from land speculators, such as General Rusk, his political enemy. He introduced bills to quiet the titles of land in the "Neutral Grounds" around Caddo Lake, and he opposed Indian legislation sponsored by Sam Houston.

In chapter two we told of the infamous Moderator-Regulator feud in the Neutral Grounds. Potter belonged to the Moderator party, which believed in law and order, enforced by the courts and legal process. This is somewhat paradoxical for Potter, in view of his behavior in North Carolina. The Regulators believed in maintaining order by vigilante action, with summary judgement, and punishment on the spot. Potter, in his new role as a Texas hero, became a leader in the Moderator party. The leader of the of the Regulators was Captain William P. Rose, "Old Rose", who lived a few miles east of Jefferson, in Caddo Bend, not far from Potter's Point. He led his men into many excesses and terrorized the law-abiding people with the threat of violence. His "kangaroo courts" usually ended in torture and death.

A stranger came to his home and asked for a match. "Old Rose" took him captive and tortured him before killing him. When the Sheriff came to arrest Rose for murder, Rose killed the Sheriff, also.

Potter decided that enough was enough, and this was too much. So, while he was in the Capitol, he had the President issue a proclamation for the arrest of Rose. Thereby, Potter, himself could legally arrest Rose. Potter must have lost his senses! Surely he must have realized that he was not any more immune to being killed by Rose than any one else!

Nevertheless, as he returned from the Capitol, he organized a posse for the purpose of arresting Rose. Although very tired from his long trip, he immediately proceeded to lead his men to Rose's home. However, Rose had learned of the posse's approach and had hidden in a pile of brush which had been stacked for burning. Rose's son, Preston, assured Potter that his father was not at home.

Potter dismissed his men for the night, and went home for a much needed night of rest. Harriet begged him to re-assemble his men for protection during the night, but he only laughed at her fears and fell asleep at once.

As dawn broke, various members of the Potter household left the house to attend to the early morning farm chores. When they failed to return at their accustomed time Harriet became alarmed and roused Potter. They realized that Rose had gathered his mob during the night and surrounded the house.

Potter decided that the best plan would be for him to make a run for the lake and hide on an island or in a cypress brake. Harriet urged him to stay and fight off the attack from inside the house, pleading that she could keep his guns reloaded as he fired at the enemy. Potter decided against this, perhaps to protect Harriet, and dashed from the house toward the lake. At the water's edge he leaned his gun against a tree and dived into the lake. The gang was in hot pursuit, and, as they reached the shore, one of them grabbed Potter's gun and fired the one shot at the back of Potter's head as he was swimming away. The men then left.

Harriet had stayed in the house; she heard the one shot, and she could hear Rose's men as they left. When Potter did not return to the house, she, and her brother, who had not been harmed when he was detained by Rose's men that morning, searched in and around the lake all day without success. Early the next day they found his body floating on the placid surface of the lake he loved.

Only two men of all his neighbors whom he had helped in their land titles dared to defy "Old Rose's" wrath and came to help bury Potter on the bluff overlooking the Lake. Thus died a great statesman, a patriot who served both the United States Navy and the Texas Navy, and was a hero in the Texas War of Independence.

As we know, Potter was a hero with feet of clay. Despite his assurances to Harriet that their marriage was legal, and despite his love for their children, he had made a will in the Capitol leaving

The cemetery where Robert Potter was initially buried on the high bluff on Potter's Point. Photo by the author, 1948.

his Potter's Point property to a Mrs. Mayfield, wife of a politician, who may have been planning to run Potter for President of the Republic.

Harriet fought for, and lived on, the property for many years; marrying Judge Charles Ames of Clarksville, a close friend of Potter's. They had several children. Harriet eventually lost her fight for the property in a decision by Chief Justice Roberts, called "infamous" by the noted authority on the life and times of Robert Potter, Mr. Samuel Asbury.

Forced from her beloved home on Potter's Point, Harriet spent her old age with her son, a medical doctor, in New Orleans. It was here, at the age 83, that Harriet wrote her autobiography from which I have quoted. Thus ended another colorful chapter in the history of Caddo Lake.

The cemetery where Potter, his daughter Lakeann, and a slave were buried is still on the bluff overlooking the lake. However, Potter's body was removed in 1936 as a part of the Texas Centennial activity by the state, for re-burial in the State Cemetery at Austin.

I visited the old cemetery several times during the '30's and '40's, searching for some trace of the Potter home, which I thought should be near the cemetery. Prior to my search a larger area had been covered, with the same intent, by a group from the University of Texas. I picked a spot which I thought offered the best view of the lake, the least likelihood of mosquitos, and the coolest breezes in summer, not far from the cemetery. One spring day I found two Iris plants in bloom right where I had pictured the front doorway of the house. Who knows? Perhaps they were planted by Harriet herself. I had found as much, or more, than anyone else has ever found of the exact location of the Potter's home.

Chapter 6

CADDO WAS...

THE TREASURE CHEST!!

Following the gradual cessation of steamboat navigation on Caddo Lake, beginning in 1873-4, the area entered a period of declining activity for about twenty years. Life on Caddo Lake had been anything but dull ever since the arrival of civilization, so, perhaps, the older people welcomed the peace and tranquillity that descended upon the lake region. Actually, the booming economy also drained away with the waters of Caddo Lake.

The river commerce, and all of the business it had brought, was gone —forever. The great plantations around the lake, which had flourished with slave labor and cheap transportation to the eastern textile mills, were now lying fallow and neglected. The Civil War and the "reconstruction" that followed had taken their vengeful toll. On the plus side, however, the stormy years of the "neutral grounds" had been cleared away by treaty. Texas' War of Independence had been won, and she had entered the Union. The Moderators and The Regulators had finally tired of their feud, and law was established. The railroad, second to be built in all of Texas, which had run from Swanson's Landing to Marshall, via Jonesville, was a victim, however, of the hard times and loss of river traffic. There just wasn't any money to circulate, and to buy the things that people couldn't make or grow for themselves.

Caddo Lake, however, was still the great natural resource of this part of the world. There was little chance of not eating well, for Caddo provided an abundance of fish, wildfowl, squirrel, rabbit, deer, and all sorts of wild game. Chinquapins, black walnuts, hickory nuts, persimmons, muscadines and wild grapes were harvested in the Fall. Mayhaws, blackberries, dewberries, wild plums, indian peaches and all sorts of things began to ripen in early Summer and were turned into the greatest jellies, jams and preserves that were ever spread on a hot biscuit or corn pone. They were equally prized when made into a liqueur.

The Caddo Lake folks lived quite well! Yet, they did require a little cash money occasionally for such things as flour, salt, nails, shot, gunpowder, fish hooks, twine, etc. They were forced to turn to commercial hunting and fishing. The commercial fishes were usually buffalo and catfish, but game fish such as "white perch" (crappie) and black bass, usually brought higher prices and were in great demand. All were easy to catch, and the supply seemed unending. The paddlefish, known locally as "spoon-bill catfish" were netted for their roe, which was rushed to eastern markets by railway in iced wooden kegs and there sold at premium price for "caviar". Ducks, geese, deer, squirrel and rabbit were hunted for both food and money.

The game laws came late to Caddo, and they were difficult to enforce. Caddo Lake was again providing for its humankind, and again was used and abused by the very people who knew it best. The lake's natural resources were being exploited and drained in a frenzy of unlawful excesses. (As of to-day, the spoon-bill catfish is so rare in Caddo Lake that when ONE is caught it rates a notice in the local newspaper, and the younger fishermen don't recognize a buffalo fish when they see one).

Now enters George Sachihiko (Ono) Murata, known as "The Jap". I don't know the real reason why George arrived at Caddo Lake. I wish I had asked him. The Japanese are noted for their love of beauty, and for their commercial fishing prowess, so perhaps Caddo Lake supplied both his interests in full measure. His first job here seems to have been as cook for an oil well drilling crew near the lake. In any event, he became a leading figure in the great pearl boom on Caddo Lake.

When the last of the Great Raft on the Red River above Shreveport had been removed, the water in Caddo Lake, which had generally been high enough to support the flourishing steamboat traffic, became lower year after year. The Big Lake diminished in size and depth until it became almost as much swamp as lake. Along the shoreline in many places, the land had such a gentle slope that it was possible to wade on the hard sandy bottom quite a distance out into the lake, and the local fishermen soon discovered that the bottom of the lake was covered with large fresh water mussels. These mussels, when removed from their shell were a handy and cheap bait for their trotlines. The Caddo Indians had thought the mother-of-pearl lining of the shells made beautiful ornaments, but soon the fishermen discovered that the mussels also produced real pearls, of some size, and great beauty. When the discovery pearl was shown to The Jap, he knew, for sure, why his gods had led him to Caddo.

Hundreds, perhaps thousands, of people joined in the search for fresh water pearls in Caddo Lake. Most of the pearling was done in Big Lake along the shoreline where the shallow water and sandy bottom made ideal habitat for pearl bearing mussels, and made it easy to take them. Usually there would be a family, or a small group of two or three people working to-gether. The gatherers would wade in water about knee deep, pulling a wooden skiff along as they went, feeling for mussel shells with their feet. When they felt a mussel, they would bend down and scoop it up with their hands and pitch it into the skiff. Many gatherers waded on hands and knees. From the shore at a distance the pearl hunters looked like hogs rooting in the mud, and so they came to be called "pearl hogs". When the skiff was filled — and one person might fill it several times a day — it was pulled to the shore and unloaded into a pile at a site used as a temporary camp. The camp was usually guarded by an elderly member of the group, who spent the day opening shells and preparing meals. At night, the entire crew opened shells by a large camp fire. At the heighth of the pearl boom, camp fires could be seen for miles all around the shores of Big Lake.

The Jap was expert at evaluating the pearls by size, shape and color. He acted as a broker, buying and selling them in quantity. Prices ranged from a few dollars up to about $1,5000.00 for the best, a small fortune in those days. George made several selling trips, going to both the east and west coasts. It is said that he became so well

"The Jap" of Caddo Lake.
Photo by the author, December 28, 1941.

known at Tiffany's in New York City that he was allowed to show his pearls over the counter to Tiffany customers. He appeared to have become relatively wealthy, and lived on the lake in style. He bought an inboard boat of some size and power, and cruised about the lake frequently. George cultivated an aura of mystery. People said that when he returned from some of these boat trips on the lake, he would show his closest friends bags of very old coins and jewelry. People thought that he had discovered buried treasure, perhaps pirate treasure, most likely LaFitte's treasure that was thought to have been hidden around Old Monterey. Still others thought that it might be a highwayman's loot, or from the safe of a sunken steamer. The Jap never divulged the source of his old coins, and would only smile in a sly but friendly way when asked if he knew of any hidden treasure around the lake. He kept the money in a paper bag on a table beside his bed when I visited him in the winter of 1942, and while I was there the man who daily brought him his newspaper came by to collect. George paid him by reaching into the bag and bringing out a hand filled to overflowing with mixed currency and coins.

The pearling industry had a short life. It ended when the first dam on Caddo Lake was built. Soon the higher water level established by the dam flooded the mussel beds so that it was no longer possible to harvest them by wading. Again, the hand of man had destroyed a way of life on Caddo Lake.

Oil —THE BLACK GOLD— replaced pearls in the treasure chest that is Caddo Lake. Oil had been discovered near the lake in Louisiana, and as drilling continued it spread to the shore of Caddo Lake. Caddo Lake was entering the twentieth century, with an oil boom developing around Oil City, Vivian, Ananias, Dixie and Mooringsport area of Caddo.

This field was one of the first large fields to be discovered in the South, second only to Spindletop field near Beaumont, Texas. It was the discovery of oil under the bed of the lake itself that caused the dam to be built on Caddo, drowning the pearl business. The drillers were trying to move their heavy machinery into a swamp lake, and they were literally bogged down. The oil moguls were exerting pressure on the government to either drain the lake and dry up the bed of the lake, or build a dam and raise the water level so that barges and power boats could take the place of the wagons and oxen or mule teams.

The dam was built on a site below Mooringsport, which had been studied by the U. S. Corps of Engineers who had determined that the soil was not suitable as the foundation for a dam. As far as I can determine, that study was not given the slightest consideration

Cable type drilling rig as used in Caddo Lake.

Photo by the author, 1941

when it was decided to build a dam. As we know, the engineers were right and the dam soon failed as water washed away the earth beneath. The cavities were filled with rubble, and Caddo Lake had a very leaky dam for many years. I, personally, have come to the conclusion that this really wasn't as bad a situation as it seemed to be, although the lake got extremely low by the end of a long hot summer, I feel that exposing the bottom to "sun baking" in the shallows helped to control the aquatic growth which now chokes the lake shallows since the new dam was built.

Caddo Lake provided one of the first locations where oil was known to be under water, and it was in Caddo Lake that the basic underwater drilling techniques so widely used all over the world to-day were first developed and used.

The first drilling in Caddo was done with "cable rigs", one of the earliest methods used for drilling a well. In Caddo Lake this involved building a large heavy and very sturdy platform over the water with a wooden derrick at one end, and a steam engine at the other. The drilling operation involved raising and lowering a large heavy "bit" on the end of a cable. The bit was made of steel with a chisel point somewhat like a star bit used for making a hole in concrete by hand. The waste chips, mud and earth were flushed out of the hole by a pumped stream of water from the lake; and this waste returned to the lake, except when samples were taken for use of the geologist. The cable rig was a very slow method of drilling under ordinary circumstances, but it was able to penetrate rock rather well, just as the star drill is used to penetrate concrete.

About this time, the rotary drilling rig was developed, and it began to be used in and around Caddo Lake. It was a great improvement —much faster, required less power, and had less down time— until the bit hit a layer of rock! Then the driller wished he had an old time cable rig, because it drilled through rock much faster. Besides that, the rotary bit had a nasty habit of just breaking up in the rock, and this meant days of down time while the crew tried to clear the hole of the drill bit pieces. No doubt you've read in the newspaper

A relic of cable drilling. Photo by the author, 1941.

that a drilling operation was shut down while the crew "fished for a tool" at the bottom of the hole.

There was a man by the name of Hughes in Shreveport who had invented and built an improved type of bit for the rotary drilling rig, which he called the "Hughes Rotary Rock Drill". Although the drillers laughed at him, each day he would put one of his rock drill bits in a "tow sack", throw the sack over his shoulder, and catch the local train, known as "the plug", from Shreveport to Oil City or Vivian. He would then go from well to well trying to persuade the driller to try out his revolutionary new bit. At first, the drillers were reluctant to give it a trial, fearing that the untried bit would break up or separate from the drill stem, and cost them days of delay. But, when the driller had run into solid rock, he was mightily tempted to test Hughes' claim that his bit would drill through the rock even faster than the old cable rig bit.

The bit worked very well, and from the trials in and around Caddo Lake, Hughes perfected his "Hughes Rotary Rock Drill". When Houston became "The Oil Capitol Of The World", Hughes moved his headquarters to Houston and called it The Hughes Tool Company. Hughes' son became even more famous than his dad, from whom he inherited the company, which expanded its business world wide. Howard Hughes became the richest man in the world during his lifetime, and his fortune derived from the rotary rock bit which got its start at Caddo Lake.

December 7, 1941 dawned as a beautiful Sunday on Caddo Lake. My wife, Loucille, and I spent the day on the lake in our boat, the ANNPAT; and came in about sundown to Shady Glade camp, where we checked out with our friend, Wally Rausheck, who was operating the camp for "Old Man" Burks Wilmore. We drove to Marshall and went to the Unique Cafe in the old tabernacle building for our usual cup of coffee and chat about the day's events on Caddo with "Red" Paslay, owner of the cafe. He told us the news that he had heard on the radio. It was "Pearl Harbor Day"!

That day ended an era — for many people, many places, many things; and the way of life on Caddo Lake would never be quite

The Jap with his radio equipment.
Photo by the author, December 28, 1941.

the same as before. Truly, those years just before "Pearl Harbor" were the very best of all. They ended too soon — but Caddo Lake survives.

After Pearl Harbor there began to be ominous talk about "The Jap" of Caddo Lake, George Murata. People said that he was sent to Caddo Lake by the Japanese government to spy on, and, perhaps, to sabotage the oil wells in the lake. "They" said that he was reporting directly to Japan via high-powered radio equipment installed in his lake house.

I determined to help George, if I could, so I went, by boat of course, to interview him for a newspaper story, with pictures. George was a U. S. citizen, honorably discharged, after years of service in the U. S. Navy. He was a real "All American Boy", but the air of mystery, which he had cultivated, had backfired. I photographed him with his radio equipment, which, far from being a "spy communications center", was just an old dry battery operated receiving set, requiring a long outside antenna to get any stations at all. Some friend had given George a huge antique power plant knife switch so George could "ground" his antenna during thunderstorms. The whole of his radio equipment was just a collection of outdated throw-away junk, spliced together with pieces of discarded, used house wiring. George had no electrical service to his house, and none was available in that location at that time. There was no more distrust of him after the article was published.

As the tragedy of Pearl Harbor changed the world and the nation, so did it , also, affect the lives of each of us. During the next four years, I had very little contact with Caddo Lake. When I did return, I learned with sorrow that you cannot go back.

Caddo Lake, and her friends, were each marked by war. And so, I feel that this should close my little story of the way...

CADDO WAS...

AUTHOR'S NOTE: Days spent in Shreveport in 1978 trying to verify the "Hughes' story" resulted in failure. Then Dr. Robert L. Koenig furnished the clue that led to success. He suggested that I visit Mr. Jones of the Jones Brothers Drilling Company in Shreveport. James Marshall Jones told me that his father, Carl Jones (deceased), had often related the story. He was a roughneck in the oil field at the time, and was very familiar with the elder Hughes efforts to get his newly invented rotary rock drill used and tested. He suggested that I contact Mr. Hubert Humphries at LSU-S. Mr. Humphries, Co-ordinator of Archives and Oral History, had taped an interview with Carl Jones, and graciously furnished me a transcript of the interview relating the Hughes story as witnessed by Mr. Carl Jones; which I have paraphrased and condensed. I am grateful to all concerned, and especially acknowledge the valuable assistance of the Oral History Collection, Louisiana State University in Shreveport, ARCHIVES. F.D.

The Caddo Diner.

Eva McCord, operator of the Caddo Diner.
Photos courtesy Maggie Williams

THE LIFE OF CADDO LAKE

"BEER BOATS"

This epistle is the result of a visit by my friend, Morley Hudson, who appeared at my door one day with the question:"Fred, what were the beer boats?".

It seems that Morley had been at Johnson's Ranch and noticed the rotting pilings across the bayou, so he asked Bob Curtis about them; and Bob, who could have told him, sent him to me. I guess I hadn't thought about them lately; but time has slipped by and many of the present Caddoans don't know what the "beer boats" were all about.

For one thing, they were a big part of that which old-timers remember as "the good old days" on Caddo Lake; especially those of us who lived in dry, dry Harrison County, also known as the "buckle on the Bible belt". The story of the bootleggers on Caddo Lake has been repeated hundreds (yea, thousands) of times, but seldom do you hear about the "beer-leggers" because they were few in number, generally poor, and not socially accepted by the wealthy distillers of rotgut. During Prohibition, the brew available to a beer drinker was as variable in quality as the locally produced booze.

All of this sets the scene for the election of Franklin D. Roosevelt, who was elected President on a Democratic Party platform which pledged repeal of the Eighteenth Amendment; the prohibition amendment. Harrison County exercised its option to stay dry. But, Marion County voted "wet" to legalize the sale of "three-two" beer. (3.2% maximum alcohol content).

At first, a lot of confusion resulted from enforcement of the law in the adjacent counties, but the net result seemed to be that it was illegal to even transport beer in Harrison County except with a Federal license which was issued only to legal beer distributors. In other words, you could not drive to Jefferson (or Longview) and bring beer to your home in Harrison County to drink it —legally.

There had to be some way to assuage the thirst of East Texas' dry counties, and, believe me, there were those on Caddo Lake who knew how! The rest of this story is about legal beer; and was obtained from the ultimate source, Eva B. McCord, who, with her husband, Alvin McCord, operated the "Caddo Diner"; first, last, and most famous of the "beer boats".

Eva, also known as "Dovie" to her close, old friends and family or "Granny" to younger friends and family, has spent most of her life on Caddo Lake. She and Alvin were commercial fishers both before and after their operation of the diner, and as most people know, most commercial fishing is done at night. If I had to bet on the person least likely to get lost in any part of Caddo Lake, day or night, wind or rain, Summer or Winter, my money would be on Dovie.

All of the old timers knew where the county boundary line was, and still is, in Caddo Lake. It was very, very important to them to know exactly, because laws in the two counties differed; not only the alcoholic drink laws, but also the game laws, including those pertaining to hunting and fishing. By act of the Texas legislature, the line is the center of the channel of Big Cypress Bayou where it runs through Caddo Lake; therefore, the tree line across the bayou in the Uncertain area was, and is, in Marion County.

The name of whomever was first with the idea is lost in the dim past, but first on the scene was the good ship "Caddo Diner", built by Bud Pyle in 1938 in Ames Springs Basin, and towed by Alvin McCord and a helper with outboard motorboats to a location on the Marion County side of Big Cypress Bayou opposite the Wolz place, which was better known as the "old log house". This was owned by an uncle of my Dad's, George Wolz. It is now known as the Fly'n Fish landing, although presently owned by Fred Petersen.

The Caddo Diner was a pontoon boat, 80 feet long by 70 feet wide. It was moored to the cypress trees forming the Marion County side of the channel, as there is no dry land on that side of the channel closer than a mile or more. The idea was that people could park their cars on the Wolz property and take a transfer boat from there to the Caddo Diner where legal beer would be served on the premises. The diner was operated for about eight months by Bessie Pyle, after which time the McCords, Alvin and Eva, took over operation.

The Caddo Diner prospered, and became one of the most popular of the dining, dancing, beer gardens in the area. It soon became evident that the eighty by seventy foot boat was too small; so, after it was torn loose from its mooring in the trees during a storm, it was hastily replaced in the same location with a one hundred by eighty foot building constructed on pilings. The Caddo Diner sign was moved to the new building, and the original boat was sold for salvage. Thus ended the hull of the one and only true "beer boat", since all of the Diner's competitors were also constructed on pilings driven into the lake bottom next to the tree line.

It was inevitable that competition would soon spring up. Floyd "Crip" Haddock built a place on pilings across from Johnson's Ranch, which he had purchased. His famous name brought even more people to the lake for real Caddo catfish and real legal beer.

Eventually, Kuehn's place was built below Crip's , and Chartier's above Caddo Diner. All were on pilings. Only the original Caddo Diner could have truly been called a boat, but the term "beer boat" has an attractive alliteration, so they were all called "beer boats". Incidentally, the pontoons on the Caddo Diner had leaked so badly that the bilge pumps had to run night and day to keep her afloat, and this was one of the reasons for replacing her with the building supported by pilings. Power was supplied to the "boats" by the rural co-op through an overhead power line from the mainland.

The Caddo Diner had all of the amenities of the standard "honky-tonk", or "beer garden" of the period. A juke box ran night and day and could be heard up and down the bayou. The machine was supplied and serviced by Mahone Amusement Co., of Marshall, owned by Ed Mahone, Jr. It took just a nickel to play a record with that deep juke box sound and see the box light up with the multicolored animated lights. Probably you've already guessed that the record that wore out the most often was "Beer Barrel Polka".

A long neck bottle of beer (no cans in those early days), regardless of brand was 15 cents. A "coke" was 5 cents. If you would like a delicious catfish dinner of fish caught the night before in Caddo Lake, you could get it in the Caddo Diner. All the whole fried catfish you could eat, with all the trimmings, would cost you 75 cents. The price of catfish "on the hoof" was 7 cents per pound. They also served steaks, chili, soup and beef stew. —And boatloads of coffee.

The Caddo Diner opened at eleven in the morning on Thursday and often stayed open continously until midnight Sunday night. The crew required eight waitresses, four cooks, and four transfer boat operators, working as two shifts, as well as Eva and Alvin. Eva insists that they called the transfer boats by that name, but most people, including myself, called them "taxi boats".

The taxi boats ran day and night, rain or shine, Summer or Winter, back and forth across the bayou. However, my wife Loucille reminds me of the time the taxi boats did not run. That winter the bayou froze solid, and a favorite pastime for a few days was skidding empty beer bottles back and forth across the bayou.

There was no charge for the taxi boat ride, though many people tipped the boatman; perhaps, a nickel or a dime. Most of the taxi boats were sixteen foot wooden flat bottom skiffs equipped with a ten horsepower Johnson or Evinrude motor. Alvin McCord built his own boats. He had four in operation. If you decided to hop over to another beer boat for whatever reason, the taxi boats, any of them, would carry you without charge, as each beer boat maintained its own fleet and things generally averaged out between them. No one ever checked to see if a passenger in the taxi ever spent any money after he arrived on the beer boat. Some just wanted a free boat ride, with better than 50/50 odds that someone would buy him a bottle of beer.

There were many good times in those carefree days. People came from all over to visit the new kind of beer garden on the water and enjoy an ice cold bottle of "Bud" or "Schlitz" or "Jax" or "Blue Ribbon", and marvel at how different it was from "home brew". Seldom could you visit a beer boat and not find a pal who wanted to swap hunting or fishing stories with you over a cold beer. The beer boats became the social center of Caddo Lake. Often noisy, there was rarely any trouble. Many men brought wives or girl friends, even children and knew that nothing would be amiss.

A long deck extended all around the front and sides of the Caddo Diner, and a special "stall" was provided for the taxi boats to load and unload passengers. Ample space was also provided for those who came in their own boats to moor them along the deck

Loucille and I often tied our "Annpat", a sixteen foot Old Town boat, with an Elto Speedster motor, to the deck of the Caddo Diner. Once, while we were docked there drinking cold "Buds" and chatting with two friends in the next stall, Loucille caught a memorable catfish. Amid screams from Loucille and much hooting and hollering from the crowd on the deck and in nearby boats she managed to "flop" the nine pounder on her bream hook and pole into the bottom of the boat, where his lively antics and flailing fins sent Loucille and I scrambling for bow and stern respectively. Moral: never let a baited hook dangle in the water while drinking a cold Bud on a hot summer afternoon. —Especially at the Caddo Diner.

The Annpat was among the first of the outboard boats on Caddo to have two-way radio and running lights, and I often cruised at night. That's the hard way on Caddo, but it's sure beautiful on a warm moonlit night. You can bet that I ran very slowly and carefully when I was in the vicinity of a beer boat. On two separate nights that I recall I have pulled couples aboard who had fallen out of a taxi boat and were floundering in the water when I arrived at the scene. The taxi pilot in each case said "They just up and jumped in the lake. I told them it was over their head!" I don't recall any drownings on a taxi boat ride, but I'll bet the taxi men could tell some wild tales about the life of a taxi boat operator for a beer boat.

The Caddo Diner had been constructed with living quarters in the rear for the McCord family, and in this way they were able to keep close tabs on the operation to make sure they stayed in compliance with the very strict laws and regulations. No hard liquor was permitted on the premises. Since ALL supplies had to be brought in by boat, this was not difficult to oversee.

The law was so strict that when the beer distributors' trucks pulled up to unload the beer on the mainland it had to be placed directly from the truck into the transfer boat. The beer could not be placed on the dock nor on the ground of Harrison County! Nor, could any of the beer make a return trip from the beer boat to the mainland (unless it was inside someone). The lawmen were vigilant and the penalties were harsh.

By 1941 the clouds of war in Europe were beginning to throw a long shadow, even onto the happy people of Caddo Lake. The "good ole days" were ebbing. The McCords decided to go back to fishing and sold their interest in the Caddo Diner to Aubry Hartzo. Three or four months later Marion County voted to go dry. The days of beer boats on Caddo Lake were over. Some attempt to operate them without the beer was made, but the magic was gone, the good ole days were but a memory; and then came the final blow, December 7, 1941, Pearl Harbor Day. America went to war in earnest, and many of us who loved Caddo knew that we loved our Nation more, and left to do our bit.

Thank you, Morley, for triggering a memory of the beer boats and the carefree days and nights of long ago.

Fred Dahmer
January 1985

THE LIFE OF CADDO LAKE

"PADS"

"What a lily pond! Must be the biggest I ever saw! But, what is all that green scum on the water"?

I've heard something similar to the above exclamation many times from visitors viewing Caddo Lake for the first time. We all understand their meaning, even though it contains some misinformation. It is nearly a mile to the nearest lily pad, and I don't ever recall observing any green scum on Caddo Lake. They are observing spatterdock pads, and duckweed pads. There's nary a lily pad in sight, and no scum!

I have no botanical training, but I've been an interested student of all plant life in, on and around Caddo for many years. Any readers who are real botanists may choose not to read further, with my blessing.

There are at least five different kinds of pads floating on the waters of Caddo Lake. Some may appear superficially alike, but the plants are quite different from each other. Also, there are several kinds of floating aquatic plants on Caddo, but this discussion will be limited to those with pads.

DUCKWEED

To some visitors this is the "green scum" which, in summer, covers a lot of the water's surface. The visitors think, seeing it from a distance, that it is the slimy green algae which grows in stagnant water. Duckweed is neither slimy, nor algae, but myriads of tiny green floating pads, each with tiny, hair-like roots suspended in the water from the center of the underside of the pad. If you scoop a handful of duckweed from the lake, it feels "gritty"; not at all slimy.

Water lily blossom and pads.

Spatterdock blossom and pads.

I do not recall seeing any duckweed on Caddo Lake until sometime around the late 1940's or 1950's, when I was told that it was "planted" in the lake by a sportsman's club in order to attract more ducks to the lake. The lady who told me this said her husband was hired by the club to do the "planting", so I consider my information credible. I have looked for, but have never seen, a duck come near it. Most of it is gone before the duck season opens on Caddo, however. It becomes rather attractive shades of reddish and purplish brown in autumn, before sinking to the bottom as the water becomes colder.

I consider the duckweed to be a weed, as its name states it to be. It proliferates in Caddo Lake uncontrolled by any known natural enemy. There is no doubt that it is a nuisance, but it seems to be a minor one at worst. I wish people would not "help" Mother Nature with Caddo Lake.

WATER LILY

In the spring, the true water lilies begin to appear. For many years, I did not see any water lilies in Caddo Lake, although I looked for them. Perhaps, there were a few and I never found the right place at the right time. Now, they are plentiful. The flowers are white, with a yellow "center", and float on the surface of the water. The pads, which also float on the surface, are circular in outline, with a narrow, wedge shaped cut to the stem in the center. Generally green in color, many are tinged, especially on the underside, in maroon and purple. The top-side of the pad has a glossy finish. Both the flower and the pad are quite attractive; the stems of both are limp and flexible, but tough. The stems are not stiff enough to support either the flower or the pad above the water's surface. They are flourishing in the vicinity of Four Forks, Turtle Shell and Old Folk's Playground, as well as elsewhere.

Water lilies are open only during the morning hours. They close up around noon. When the blossom has finished blooming, the seeds begin to form, and the flexible stem contracts into a "corkscrew", which draws the flower some distance under water, where the seeds are eventually released to be spread by the water currents.

SPATTERDOCK

The first pad to appear in the spring is the spatterdock. This ubiquitous plant grows almost everywhere on this continent where water is found. The young pads closely resemble those of the water lily, and it is difficult to tell which is which, unless they are growing close to-gether. The pads are cut, like those of the water lily, but are a more yellowish green, with a shiny "waxed" appearance. The flowers, at first glance, seem to be ball-shaped yellow knots elevated an inch or two above the water. When closely examined, we can see the yellow petals almost totally enclosed by the green sepals. The petals close over the top of the flower, making the ball shape and concealing the curiously shaped center. The roots of spatterdock are embedded in the bottom of the lake, growing out of a stalk resembling a large banana stalk, which lies horizontally on the bottom. The pad stems and the flower stems grow upward from this same stalk. When the water becomes cold in the winter, the flowers and most of the pads die, and then the stalks come free of the roots and float to the surface of the lake. When this happened the "old timers" would say the "lake is turning over", and mark their calenders. For some reason not very clear to me they placed great significance in this event, and the date on which it occurred.

The spatterdock becomes a nuisance in warm weather because it grows so profusely. The pads often overlap on top of the water, and the stems intertwine beneath, forming an impenetrable barrier to boat propellors as well as fishing lures. I'd hate to see them all gone, but Caddo Lake could do with a few trillion less. PLEASE don't call them "lily pads"!

GOLDEN CLUB

There is one plant in Caddo that you can't mistake, with its curious floating pads that are spear shaped, about one inch wide, perhaps four inches long, and a beautiful bronze color. This plant, whose thin stems end in roots in the lake bottom, grows only in running water. The stems of the pads are far too weak to support the weight of the pads in air, but anchor the floating pads against the pull of the water's current. This is the golden club, so named for the yellow-gold, white tipped flower spike which appears briefly in early summer. This "club" protrudes a few inches above the water, and is about finger size and shape. It is worth looking at closely if you can hold the boat in place in the running water. As with all wildflowers, it should not be picked, or pulled up. In former days, when I fished a good bit, we would catch "white perch" in the Towhead vicinity by just letting our hooked minnow dangle in the water as the boat drifted through clumps of goldenclub. Goldenclub is a great asset to Caddo Lake, and there would never be enough of it to cause anyone the slightest trouble.

YONQUPIN

The crowning glory of Caddo Lake is the yonqupin, rating right alongside cypress trees and spanish moss as a feature attraction of the lake. Let's get the controversy over the spelling of this name out of our way right now. The more common and better known name for this beauty is American lotus. The name "yonqupin" is a colloquialism, and you won't find it in WEBSTER'S SEVENTH NEW COLLEGIATE DICTIONARY. It is, however, in WEBSTER'S THIRD NEW INTERNATIONAL DICTIONARY, UNABRIDGED. (That's the big one!) In this book, it is spelled "yoncopin", defined as "water chinquapin". I have seen it spelled other ways in various botanical books. Since the word is a colloquial one, I feel I have some freedom in the way I choose to spell it, and many years ago, I made the choice to spell the word yonqupin because in lower case type characters the letters "q" and "p" resemble the plant's pads, held high above the water on sturdy stems. Please note that the plant is a lotus, NOT a lily! The yonqupin pads begin to reach their full growth in late summer, and this is when the buds open and the flowers spread into glorious full bloom.

The bluish-green pads may be enormous; some must reach two feet in diameter; some float on the surface of the water and some

Yonqupin blossom.
Photo by author.

are raised on long hard stems a foot or more above the water. The upper surface of the pad has a dull, or matte, finish, upon which drops of water ball up and refract the light with a gem-like sparkle in vivid contrast to the pad's dull surface. The large flowers are a creamy yellow color, with massive petals that open wide surrounding the large structure which will house the seeds long after the flower petals wither away.

The seed receptacle is highly prized, when dry, as a decorator item or ornament. I've been told that the dried seed pods sell for $1.00 each in the large cities, especially during the holiday season. The area around Uncertain has been harvested for several seasons now by commercial people who gather about 99% of the seed pods, leaving only defective ones. Sometimes they use airboats for this purpose, and can cover a great territory in a short time. There is now a hefty fine if they can be caught in possession of the pods, with possible attachment of the boat, in addition.

The seeds themselves resemble chinquapins, or acorns, and are edible if harvested in their prime, just before they begin to dry out. They taste like chesnuts. The roots are also edible and are usually prepared as a sort of casserole.

I must confess that I am among those who get disturbed at all the pads in the lake when my motor bogs down in them. I've seen them so thick that it was nearly impossible to push a canoe through them. I have, also, seen the pads sprayed with weed-killer, and was glad of it until I saw the result: rotted and horribly deformed plants; a sickening sight coupled with the foul stench of rotten vegetation; mixed with the acrid smell of the poisonous chemical spray, which lingers in the air for weeks after.

In light of the alternative, I have come to the conclusion that the pads aren't so bad after all. They furnish ideal shade and shelter, for fish, and for the marine life upon which the fish feed. I have decided that it is probably stupid to try to bulldoze a boat through them, anyway. I've concluded that the pads and their blossoms, in their own way, are only adding to the beauty and enjoyment of Caddo.

These pads were not always so plentiful in Caddo Lake, as shown by most of the pictures of the lake taken in the old days. In fact, as I look through my older pictures of the lake, I am struck by the "bareness" of the lake, almost like a bare-faced youth. Modern photos show the lush semi-tropical growth; the true beauty of maturity, which we take for granted, to-day. In all candor, I do believe the fishing is better to-day, especially for game fish.

In fact, I am just about to give utterance to what some people may consider the ultimate heresy: I do believe that Caddo Lake, to-day, is the best I've ever seen it! Let's keep it that way!

Ames Springs Basin, Caddo Lake.

THE LIFE OF CADDO LAKE

"POETRY"

I once lived next door to the grandest neighbor any person could ever have. Lisbeth Spivey, wife of J. D. Spivey, lived in "Dummy" Albright's old house. She loved Caddo Lake, and all of the living things connected with the lake.

Daniel W. Albright at the linotype machine he once operated.

Among the many nice things she did for me was to give me a copy of her diary about her life on Caddo Lake; and a copy of some poems written by Daniel W. Albright, the deaf mute, who was widely known in these parts as "Dummy". Dummy's handicap made "real time" communication difficult for him, but I believe his poems give us an insight into the strange, lonely, silent world in which he spent his days and nights as a Caddo Lake commercial fisherman and fishing camp owner.

From his poems you would scarcely guess that he was deaf. Amongst his papers, I found one in which he explained that he could sense, or "feel", certain sounds.

As in a:

THUNDERSTORM
Again, we view
Jehovah's wrath
As Nature clears
For him a path.

Roaring thunders!
Lightning's flash!
Fearsome - blinding
is their crash.

* * *

JUPE
I am Jupe, a mighty God.
I rule the world above —
And yet, for all my warlike mein,
I, too, can show some love.

I bring relief to parching earth,
revive the dying flowers;
I pour, as in the hardest rain,
Or light as Springtime showers.

And with my crashing thunderbolts
I clear the skies for you.
So, still your thoughtless curse, my friend,
And give old Jupe his due.

* * *

"Poetry"

Dummy loved to go duck hunting:

> A lonely duck in some place flight
> Paused just a sec to see —
> What manner of ducks sat down there
> As quiet as quiet could be.
>
> That lonely duck in some place flight
> No longer the air will cleave.
> From those quiet ducks down below
> An A-bomb seemed to heave.

* * *

Many years later, he wrote:

THEN AND NOW

> I watch those swirling banners
> As the chilling winds rush past.
> In my heart there is a longing
> For those days that went so fast.
>
> Those days when in a duck-blind,
> I shivered through each bone,
> Watching ducks light by hundreds —
> And no mud-hens came alone.

* * *

The fish peddling truck, with some of Dummy's family and friends.

Dan sold fish to a "broker" when he could, but if the broker wasn't buying, and the fish wouldn't keep, he peddled them, himself:

MY PEDDLING DAYS

Those days of old,
Those days of gold,
Those days we knew so
    well.

Those days of old,
When fish we sold,
Those days when we
    played hell.

Those days of old,
When our moral mold
Was such, no truth we'd
    tell.

Those days of old,
When harps we'd fold,
Just so our fish to sell.

* * *

70

"Poetry"

*Dummy's family on the bridge which they built
to their home on Taylor Island.*

Some of his poems were just for fun:

CATFISH DOINGS
Big cat meets up with little cat.
The two— they swim a jig —
Roam through Davy's locker,
Dance on Blackbeard's brig!

* * *

71

Or, in a solemn mood:

THE DAY ON CADDO

Down Caddo way, as you drift along,
Making a cast, or humming a song,
The Spanish moss above you waves,
Hoary with memories of forgotten graves.
And as you pass, in progress slow,
It seems to murmur, "Mortals, they go
In search of pleasure, frolic or fun;
Then join those whose 'day is done'."

* * *

Or, the epilogue to:

THE DAY ON CADDO

But the Spanish moss, with its roll and wave,
And all the legends of forgotten grave,
Can never take from the joy of the day
Spent on Caddo — down our way.

* * *

The elements were a powerful force in his life, and he wrote
about them:

NATURE'S APRIL FOOL

Again that Spanish moss's a-wave,
A-roll, a-swirl, a-toss;
As though in mourning for a soul
That to the world's a loss.

As we watch the northern breeze,
A-swing, a-sway, a-tool,
We view in wonder Nature's prank —
A chilly "April Fool".

* * *

"Poetry"

A banshee wail is in my ears;
Dead leaves go flying past.
The witches ride this Halloween
With a norther crowding fast.

* * *

Sodom and Gomorrah were "hot", they say,
But they had nothing on Caddo to-day.
This sizzling sunlight, with glare so fierce,
Right through my eyeballs does probe and
pierce.
And the fan on the dresser, whirling around,
Has, for me, very little of comfort found.

* * *

Howl, ye blustery north wind, howl;
Prowl, ye four-footed slinking varmints, prowl;
Seeking, perchance, a bone, a crust of bread?
A sheltered cranny for a bed?

Safe am I, in my Father's care;
Fearing no danger from "out there".
Through my lonely nights and days,
His protection enfolds me always.

Fain would I have my Dear One with me,
His touch to feel, His smile to see.
What would matter, wind or weather,
Could we two only be together?

* * *

73

I have heard this same wildcat scream, lying abed late at night, many years ago. Dummy couldn't really hear it, but his poem is a vivid description:

>Down on Caddo — t'other night,
>Full in the moonlight shining bright,
>A furry form — long and sleek —
>With our dogs played hide'n seek.
>That feline form was seen by none,
>But, footprints showed when night was done.
>Also, was heard its unearthly screech —
>Deprived our womenfolks of speech!
>It rambled in — then rambled out.
>They say it was a catamount.

On another awesome denizen of Caddo:

>Mighty was I in the olden days,
>When I roamed the Caddo waterways.
>In these jaws with clamp of steel,
>Weight of a hundred-fold you'd feel.
>All was meat unto this maw,
>I'd dine on fish — or from a leg of "pa".
>Now, helpless I lie, that you may view;
>And give to a loggerhead its due.
>
>* * *

Or, less fearsome:

FROGS

>When the sack breaks you find 'em —
>In the parlor, in the sink,
>In the bucket whereat you drink —
>In the attic, on the roof,
>By that time you're goofy — POOF!
>
>* * *

CRAWFISH

Lives there a guy, with humor so dead,
Who never to his pal has said:
"I put a crawfish down her neck;
And got a black eye, I did, by heck."

* * *

NEARER, NEARER

Nearer, nearer, the waters creep.
I'm skeered of those denizens of the deep;
The minnow with its darting ways,
Never in one place it stays.

The lurking turtle, round and fat,
Biteth tootsies, thin and flat.
I'm skeered of those monsters of the deep,
As nearer, nearer, the waters creep.

* * *

Dummy was a fisherman:

"I hate 'em, I hate 'em!"
Those motors that swirl
Up alongside, and dampen my girl.

"I hate 'em, I hate 'em!"
The drivers of same,
Who lack the rudiments of playing the game.

* * *

But, years later, he wrote:

I hated 'em, I hated 'em, indeed I did,
Those motorized bathtubs with their roar and skid,
And their asinine driver — call him whatever you
    wish —
Who bawls as he passes: "You catchin' any fish?"

But time alters viewpoint; what wouldn't I give
For a single day in which I could live,
Rocked by his wave, drenched by his spray, gratifying
    a wish,
Hearing him bellow: "You catchin' any fish?"

* * *

FISHERMAN'S COMPLAINT

As we homewards hie from a day well spent,
With thinned out purse, and pants a-rent,

Through our minds they drift and pass,
The "kerchug" of plug, and strike of bass.

* * *

A speedboat race on Caddo Lake described in Dummy's poem.
Photo by the author.

Dummy loved speedboating, too:

THE SPEEDBOAT RACE (IN A JAM)
Stingin spray and flying spume!
We pound, we rock, swerve and zoom,
Roaring motors deafening ears;
Death by inches now appears.

Demons each side; wakes we crest;
"Now I lay me —" and all the rest;
Sickening swerve — death now looms;
Out from under, a speeder zooms.

One right behind — "on your tail",
Pray your motor does not fail.
God! "Someone has overturned",
Swiftly swerving, past we've churned!

Never slowing — throttle wide!
— It's for the judges to decide!

* * *

Very few people realized that Dummy was, also, a sensitive and lonely person:

Old "Spanish" nods with a gentler wave,
To the top of a hill and a new made grave,
And the rippling waters going past,
Seemingly murmur — "Aye, they're going fast".

* * *

THE LIFE OF CADDO LAKE

Again in retrospect I go,
Back to those days of long ago.
In my thoughts as tho' in stride,
Again a form stands by my side.

That form, it is no longer here;
It's on a hill top very near,
And all around it there are weeds,
Where lack of love breeds "neglect" seeds.

* * *

Selected and edited from a collection of the poems of Daniel W. (Dummy) Albright.

Fred Dahmer

A boat from Mooringsport, Louisiana in Big Cypress bayou returning from a trip to Jefferson, Texas. July, 1941. Photo by the author.

"Jackfish Alley" in Mossy Brake. Photo by the author.

Fishing in Mossy Brake near "The Art Gallery".

CADDO WAS...

SOURCES, ETC.

I have tried to confine this history to Caddo Lake and its shores, digressing only to discuss the factors that I deem vital to a full understanding of my subject. As stated in the text, source documentation on Caddo Lake history is nearly nonexistent. In my files are many clippings on Caddo Lake. Much of this material is obviously incorrect. Of the little remaining material, some is so doubtful that I would hesitate to use it; and some would verify what I already knew. I do not consider any of it to be *source* material.

1. Jesse Ivir Carter (deceased): A sober, serious man; not given to jokes or fiction; a bank president who loved Caddo and knew it well; who was always careful, when discussing Caddo with a favorite nephew, to separate fact from fiction.

2. Eva B. McCord (deceased): A prime source for the chapter on beer boats, and longtime resident on Caddo Lake.

3. R. W. Rausheck: Grew to manhood on Caddo Lake; his father was the game warden; Worked for the Johnson Brothers at their "ranch"; worked for Burks Wilmore, Sr. at the original Shady Glade fishing camp; a primary source.

4. U. S. Army Corps of Engineers: *Reports of 1873-1874*, New Orleans District.

5. Harriet (Moore Page Potter) Ames: *The History of Harriet Ames*. A copy in the possesion of Bill Haggard, owner of Lakeview Lodge, in January 1946.

6. Taped *interview with Carl Jones*. Oral History Collection, Louisiana State University, ARCHIVES, Shreveport, Louisiana.

CADDO WAS ...

Highly recommended reading dealing with the history of the two largest towns nearest Caddo Lake:

Jefferson: Riverport to the Southwest, by Fred Tarpley. Eakin Press, Austin, Texas.

Shreveport, The Beginnings, by Holice H. Henrici. University of Southwestern Louisiana, Lafayette, Louisiana.

The author, Fred Dahmer, making more memories of his *Caddo Lake*.